RESCUE AND RECOVERY DIVER:
12 THINGS TO KNOW

by Samantha S. Bell

STORY LIBRARY
MORE TO EXPLORE

www.12StoryLibrary.com

12-Story Library is an imprint of Bookstaves.

Developed and produced for 12-Story Library by Focus Strategic Communications Inc.

Library of Congress Cataloging-in-Publication Data
Names: Bell, Samantha, author.
Title: Rescue and recovery diver : 12 things to know / by Samantha S. Bell.
Description: Mankato, Minnesota : 12-Story Library, [2022] | Series: Daring and dangerous jobs |
Includes bibliographical references and index. | Audience: Ages 10–13 | Audience: Grades 4–6
Identifiers: LCCN 2020016110 (print) | LCCN 2020016111 (ebook) | ISBN 9781632359421 (library binding) |
ISBN 9781632359773 (paperback) | ISBN 9781645821076 (pdf)
Subjects: LCSH: Divers—Juvenile literature. | Search and rescue operations—Juvenile literature. |
Diving—Juvenile literature.
Classification: LCC GV840.S78 B36 2022 (print) | LCC GV840.S78 (ebook) | DDC 797.2/3—dc23
LC record available at https://lccn.loc.gov/2020016110
LC ebook record available at https://lccn.loc.gov/2020016111

About the Cover

A diver searches a canal in St. Petersburg, Russia.

Access free, up-to-date content on this topic plus a full digital version of this book. Scan the QR code on page 31 or use your school's login at 12StoryLibrary.com.

Table of Contents

Divers Save Lives

Crash-landing an aircraft on water is known as ditching.

Rescue and recovery divers search for people who are trapped underwater. They must be ready to help in different kinds of emergencies. Sometimes an airplane will crash into the water. Other times, two boats will collide. The people on board may be trapped. The plane or boat may begin to sink. Rescue divers respond right away. They assess the situation. Then they work to bring the people back to safety.

Sometimes recreational divers can have diving accidents. These include coming up too fast or running out of air. Some divers panic and lose control. They can get lost and not be able to find their way back. Rescue divers

must be ready to help these divers. They must understand the environment and how it affects a diver's safety. They must also be ready to help themselves.

Divers help other divers.

3

Number of people rescued by Chinese diver Zhong Haifeng

- In November 2017, a cargo ship sank another ship in Guangzhou Port, China.
- Zhong was in charge of the search for survivors, and he dived many times.
- He was presented the International Maritime Organization Award for Exceptional Bravery at Sea.

2

Recovery Divers Find Things that Are Lost

During a recovery mission, divers aren't trying to save a human life. Sometimes they are searching for an object. The object may be as big as a missing plane or boat. Sometimes they search for stolen or missing vehicles.

Recovering lost vehicles swamped by flood waters is a common task for divers.

Some recovery divers are trained to collect evidence used in a crime. Sometimes criminals throw their weapons into the water to get rid of them. Recovery divers look for knives, guns, and bullets. They often find them in lakes and ponds. In this way, they help put criminals in jail.

6

Sometimes recovery divers look for a person who has already died. The person may have been the victim of a crime. The person may have drowned in a lake, river, or the ocean. Finding the person is a very difficult mission. But it is important to the victim's family and community.

Rescue missions take place even in terrible conditions.

3

Rescue and Recovery Divers Need Extra Training

Training courses sharpen divers' skills.

A diver may have a lot of experience. But they will need extra training to become a certified rescue and recovery diver. The training depends on the instructor. However, there are skills every rescue and recovery diver needs.

Because it can be hard to see underwater, divers must be able to do many things without looking.

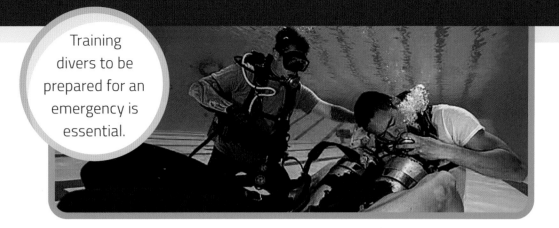

Training divers to be prepared for an emergency is essential.

These include handling their own or another diver's equipment. They must be able to go down and come back up safely. They must also be able to get themselves and others untangled.

Some of the training is in a classroom, such as learning CPR and first aid. Some training requires practicing in a pool.

THINK ABOUT IT

The more divers practice for emergencies, the more prepared they will be. How do you practice for emergencies?

For example, divers may practice by searching for a fake gun. They practice finding and bringing up people. They practice handling situations with their mask off or flooded with water.

12

Minimum age for rescue diver training with PADI

- PADI stands for the "Professional Association of Diving Instructors."
- PADI offers a junior adventure diver program.
- Young divers must have already completed the regular diving course.

9

Rescue Divers Search through Caves

Cave diving is extremely dangerous because of poor visibility and strong currents.

Some underwater cave systems are natural. Others are human-made, such as flooded mines or passageways. Some divers like to go in these caves. But if they get lost or trapped, it's very difficult to get them out. Even rescue divers with a lot of experience in open water are not

prepared to go in caves. They need specialized training and equipment.

Most of the time, their missions are recovery missions. The recovery divers must take extra steps to bring a victim out of a cave. First, they use photos and videos to record the victim and the location. This information helps the rescue team make a plan before they start. They don't want to risk the life of the recovery divers.

INTERNATIONAL UNDERWATER CAVE RESCUE AND RECOVERY (IUCRR)

The IUCRR began in 1982 in Florida. A police officer saw the need for specially trained cave divers. Today, the IUCRR is an international volunteer organization. Its members work with police to recover victims.

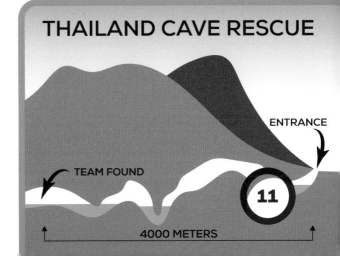

THAILAND CAVE RESCUE

ENTRANCE

TEAM FOUND

11

4000 METERS

Rescue and Recovery Divers Are Also Public Servants

Police, fire, and rescue forces often work together cooperatively.

Many of the rescue and recovery divers are also firefighters and police officers. Teams form within the departments. Some already know how to dive, while others are just learning. But they all must go through special training.

Depending on where they are located, the roles of police and firefighter divers may be different. Firefighters can often get to a location faster. They respond to emergencies as rescue divers. Many divers with the police department work as recovery divers. They gather evidence. They investigate underwater crime scenes. They keep the area secure.

In some cities, the departments work separately. In other cities, they work together. Sometimes

Divers save the lives of victims and recover vehicles.

one department starts the rescue or recovery operation, and the other one finishes it. They share their equipment and resources.

THINK ABOUT IT

Think of a time you worked with someone to complete a task. Did it make the task easier to do?

1988

Year the National Academy of Police Diving (NAPD) was formed

- The NAPD was created by a group of police divers.
- They wanted a national standard for training and certification.
- The NAPD teaches divers basic skills as well as criminal investigation techniques.

13

Rescue and Recovery Divers Need a Lot of Equipment

Divers use many types of specialty gear.

balance underwater. Regulators allow divers to breathe underwater.

Rescue and recovery divers need special gear, too. Dry suits protect them in cold water. The suits keep them completely dry. Full face masks cover the diver's face. Some have microphones

Rescue and recovery divers use basic scuba gear. This includes a Buoyancy Control Device (BCD). Divers use the BCD to control how high or low they float in the water. Weight belts help them get their

Hazmat suits protect divers from hazardous materials.

$3,000
Cost of a hazmat diving suit

- Sometimes harmful chemicals are in the water.
- This can happen if a car goes off the road or a boat tips over.
- A hazmat diving suit protects the divers from the chemicals.

and headphones. That way, the diver can communicate.

The divers also use a lot of other equipment. They may use metal detectors to find metal objects. Sometimes they use underwater cameras. They need trucks and trailers to help them get boats to search locations.

UNDERWATER IMAGES

Some dive teams use side scan sonar. This allows them to search a large area quickly. It gives them a picture of the object at the bottom of a lake, river, or ocean. It can even help divers find missing people in time.

Sonar equipment allows teams to search large areas quickly.

15

Recovery Divers Work as a Team

Sometimes recovery divers go into dark water. Working as a team helps them stay safe. The team is made up of three divers. The primary diver does the search. The back-up diver waits in full gear. This diver is ready to help if the primary diver gets into trouble. The third diver is dressed except for mask and fins. All three divers are tied with a communications rope.

The search leader is called the *tender.* The tender controls the rope. Some ropes have

All members of the dive team have to cooperate and work as a unit.

communication lines. They connect to microphones and headphones in the diver's mask. The tender and diver can talk to each other. Sometimes the tender uses the rope itself to signal the diver.

KEEPING TRACK

The profiler is another member of the dive team. Profilers record the search. They use maps to keep track of where the divers have been. That way, they can make sure every area is covered.

60 or less
Number of seconds it takes for a back-up diver to reach the primary diver

- Tenders use the rope to give directions.
- They can tell the divers which way to go.
- The diver can use the rope to signal for help.

Sometimes Divers Work in Total Darkness

Water can be so dark and murky that even powerful diving lights don't help.

Sometimes the water is too dark for divers to see anything. They may be diving at night. They may be diving in polluted water. When there is no visibility, it is called *black water*. In black water, divers must search by feeling. Often they are searching for something on the bottom, such as a cellphone or bullet.

The dangers divers face increase in the darkness. It's easier for divers to become tangled in barbed wire or treetops. They can cut

Divers train for low visibility work by using blacked out masks.

themselves on sharp objects. They may swim into enclosed areas without knowing it. They don't know where they have been or where they need to go. The other members of the dive team help from the boat.

Divers need special training for black water diving. They need to be able to do everything without being able to see. These include handling the equipment and dealing with emergencies. They must also be able to rescue another diver.

0
Percent of visibility in black water training

- Divers may start off in a swimming pool with their masks blacked out.
- Then they move to open water with their masks blacked out.
- Eventually they move to real black water conditions.

Rescue and Recovery Divers Risk Their Health

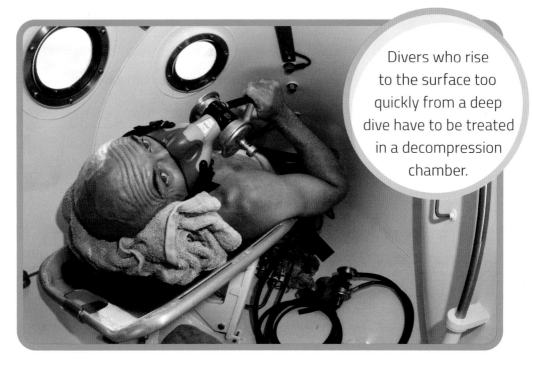

Divers who rise to the surface too quickly from a deep dive have to be treated in a decompression chamber.

All divers face health risks. Some suffer from barotrauma if they dive down too fast. Barotrauma occurs when pressure in the middle ear decreases. This causes damage and pain. Sometimes divers come up too quickly. The change in pressure creates nitrogen bubbles inside their tissues. This is called decompression sickness.

80

Depth in feet (24 m) at which a diver can experience nitrogen narcosis

- Too much nitrogen can also cause nitrogen narcosis.
- Narcosis makes a diver feel drowsy or giddy.
- It can cause the diver to make poor decisions.

Coming up from deep dives must be done in stages to avoid injury.

It can cause joint pain or even paralysis.

Rescue and recovery divers face other dangers as well. For example, they may be diving at the site of a boating accident.

The water may have gasoline or other chemicals in it. There may be sharp pieces of boats or tangled wires. Or they may be searching dark water for criminal evidence. The divers must decide if it is worth the risk.

WORKING THROUGH IT

Rescue and recovery divers face many difficult situations. Sometimes they work alone in total darkness. They bring up people who have drowned. They must be careful with criminal evidence. The divers must be able to deal with the stress.

Rescue and Recovery Divers Risk Their Lives

Rescue and recovery divers face many dangers. Often the divers can't see where they are going. The water may be polluted. Currents can be very strong. The divers can get trapped in a cave or under ice. They can get cut on broken glass or jagged pieces of metal. Sometimes divers get tangled up underwater.

Diving under ice can be hazardous because it is easy to get lost.

Some get caught in fish habitats. The habitats are created for sports fishing. Some have human-made trees in all shapes,

40

Number of minutes it took to rescue the girl who fell off a bridge in Pompey, NY

- In June 2019, a 15-year-old girl fell into a cold, fast-moving creek.
- She held onto a firefighter's hand until a rescue diver could reach her.
- The diver fought the current, darkness, and rain.

sizes, and materials. Divers can also become entangled in the communication rope or other gear. They can get caught in a type of seaweed called *kelp*. If they don't get free in time, they run out of air.

RISK A LOT TO SAVE A LOT

Divers must decide how much risk they will take. For example, many divers will go into dangerous water to save a child. But they may not take that risk just to bring up an object.

Rescue and Recovery Divers Help during Boating Accidents

Sometimes boats have accidents on the water. A boat can catch on fire. It may crash into another boat. A boat can begin to leak. Bad weather can cause it to sink. When accidents occur, rescue and recovery divers move into action.

In September 2019, 33 recreational divers boarded a boat called the

MV Conception burst into flame off the coast of Santa Cruz, California.

5
Number of crew members who survived the *Conception* fire

- One crew member was supposed to be on night watch.
- They were all asleep when the fire started.
- There was no way they could save the divers.

MV Conception. They went on a night dive. But after they went to bed, a fire broke out. It may have started because too many electrical devices were charging.

Rescue divers traveled through thick fog to reach the boat. They were expecting to rescue a lot of people. But the divers had been asleep below the deck. They all died in the fire. One crew member died, too. The rescue mission became a recovery mission.

THINK ABOUT IT

Sometimes accidents like the boat fire happen. But people should still take steps to stay safe. What are some things you do to stay safe?

Rescue and Recovery Divers Use Technology

Some robots are remote-operated vehicles (ROV). They can be as small as a computer or as big as a small truck. ROVs are usually tied to a boat with a special cable. Divers control the ROV through the line. Most ROVs have a still camera, video camera, and lights. They transmit the images back to the ship. Some ROVs have robotic arms that can lift, grab, and cut.

Some dive teams have underwater robots. The robots can stay underwater longer. They are also not affected by cold water. Divers use the robots to access a situation before they dive. The robot can take sonar images of objects underwater. That way, the divers know if they should go down or keep looking.

The 2011 tsunami and earthquake destroyed more than 120,000 homes.

Divers must be careful when using ROV in areas with fast currents. The ROV may drift in the current.

The cable can become tangled with other objects under the water.

The Japan Coast Guard was founded in 1948 and has a staff of 12,000.

2011
Year an earthquake and tsunami hit Tohoku, Japan

- The earthquake caused the giant 130-foot (40 m) wave that hit the city.
- Thousands of people were killed.
- The Japan Coast Guard used underwater robots to look for victims.

More Daring and Dangerous Jobs

Underwater Welder

Some divers are underwater welders. They repair things underwater such as pipelines, dams, and ships. If possible, dry chambers are created underwater. That way, the welders can concentrate on the job.

Deadhead Logger

During the 19th century, many loggers in the US transported trees on the waterways. Some of the trees were lost underwater. Today, deadhead loggers dive to find the valuable trees. They deal with wild animals such as sharks, venomous snakes, and alligators.

Hazmat Diver

Hazmat divers dive into water that contains hazardous materials or dangerous chemicals. These can include raw sewage or paper pulp. It can include fuel after a boating accident. Hazmat divers assess the situation. Then they decide on a plan to clean it up.

Glossary

cargo ship
A boat that carries goods from one place to another.

certified
Officially recognized as having certain skills.

collide
To run into something while moving.

CPR
An emergency procedure performed when someone's heart stops beating.

current
The strong flowing movement of water.

habitat
The place where an animal or plant lives.

hazmat
Short for hazardous materials.

metal detector
A machine that uses an electromagnetic field to locate metal objects.

nitrogen
A colorless, odorless gas that makes up 3 percent of the human body.

paralysis
The inability to move part or most of the body.

sonar
A system for finding objects underwater by bouncing sound waves off them.

Read More

Aronson, Marc. *Rising Water: The Story of the Thai Cave Rescue.*, New York, NY: Simon & Schuster, 2019.

Savage, Jeff. *Deadly Hard-Hitting Sports*. Minneapolis, MN: Lerner Publishing, 2013.

Swanson, Jennifer. *Astronaut-Aquanaut: How Space Science and Sea Science Interact* Washington, DC: National Geographic Kids, 2018.

Visit 12StoryLibrary.com

Scan the code or use your school's login at **12StoryLibrary.com** for recent updates about this topic and a full digital version of this book. Enjoy free access to:

- Digital ebook
- Breaking news updates
- Live content feeds
- Videos, interactive maps, and graphics
- Additional web resources

Note to educators: Visit 12StoryLibrary.com/register to sign up for free premium website access. Enjoy live content plus a full digital version of every 12-Story Library book you own for every student at your school.

Index

About the Author

Samantha S. Bell has written more than 125 nonfiction books for children. She also teaches art and creative writing to children and adults. She lives in the Carolinas with her family and too many cats.